It's Catching

Mumps

Elizabeth Laskey

© 2003 Reed Educational & Professional Publishing
Published by Heinemann Library,
an imprint of Reed Educational & Professional Publishing,
Chicago, Illinois
Customer Service 888-454-2279
Visit our website at www.heinemannlibrary.com

Designed by Patricia Stevenson
Printed and bound in the United States by Lake Book Manufacturing

07 06 05 04 03
10 9 8 7 6 5 4 3 2 1

Library of Congress Cataloging-in-Publication Data
Laskey, Elizabeth, 1961–
    Mumps / Elizabeth Laskey.
        v. cm. — (It's catching)
    Includes bibliographical references and index.
    Contents: What is mumps? — Healthy nose and throat —
    What causes mumps? — First signs — The next stage —
    How mumps is spread — Treatment — Feeling better —
    When mumps is more serious — Avoiding mumps —
    Getting a mumps vaccine — Staying healthy — Think about it.
    ISBN 1-4034-0275-2
    1. Mumps—Juvenile literature. [1. Mumps. 2. Diseases.]
    I. Title. II. Series.

    RC168.M8 L37 2002
    616.3'13—dc21

                           2001008564

Acknowledgments
The author and publishers are grateful to the following for permission to reproduce copyright material:
Cover photograph by Mauritius, GMBH/PhotoTak
p. 4 Clinica Claros/PhotoTake; pp. 5, 17 Bob Daemmrich/Stock Boston, Inc.; p. 6 Blair Seitz/Photo Researchers, Inc.; p. 7 Mary Kate Denny/PhotoEdit/PictureQuest; p. 8 Oliver Meckes/Gelderblom/Photo Researchers, Inc.; p. 9 John Lei/Stock Boston, Inc.; pp. 10, 14 Visuals Unlimited; p. 11 Oscar Burriel/Science Photo Library/Photo Researchers, Inc.; p. 12 Frank Siteman/Stock Boston, Inc.; p. 13 Ariel Skelley/Corbis Stock Market; p. 15 Relections Photo Library/Corbis; p. 16 David M. Grossman/Photo Researchers, Inc.; p. 18 Mauritius/GMBH/PhotoTake; p. 19 Bill Truslow/Stock Connection/PictureQuest; p. 20 Michael W. Thomas/Focus Group/PictureQuest; p. 21 David M. Grossman/PhotoTake; p. 22 Susan Leavines/Photo Researchers, Inc.; p. 23 Tom and Dee Ann McCarthy/Corbis Stock Market; p. 24 Saturn Stills/Science Photo Library/Photo Researchers, Inc.; p. 25 Bob Krist/Corbis; p. 26 Education Images Ltd./Custom Medical Stock Photo, Inc.; p. 27 Tim Pannell/Corbis Stock Market; p. 28 Michael Newman/PhotoEdit; p. 29 Biophoto Associates/Science Source/Photo Researchers, Inc.
Every effort has been made to contact copyright holders of any material reproduced in this book. Any omissions will be rectified in subsequent printings if notice is given to the publisher.

Some words are shown in bold, **like this.** You can find out what they mean by looking in the glossary.

Contents

What Is Mumps?

Mumps is an illness that causes your cheeks to puff out and **swell.** The area around your **jaw** may also swell.

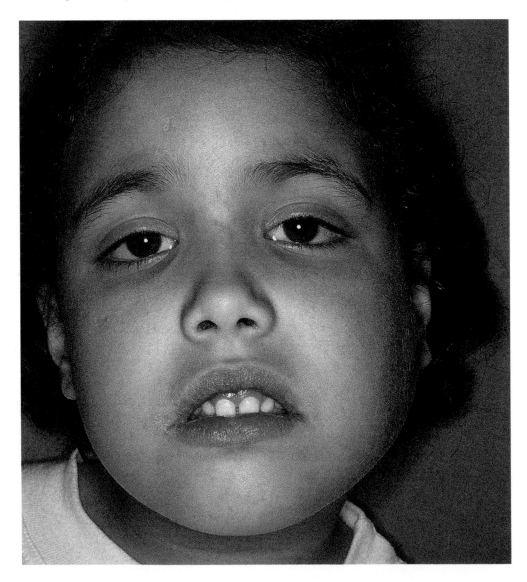

Mumps is an **infectious** illness. This means it can spread from one person to another by being close or sharing a glass.

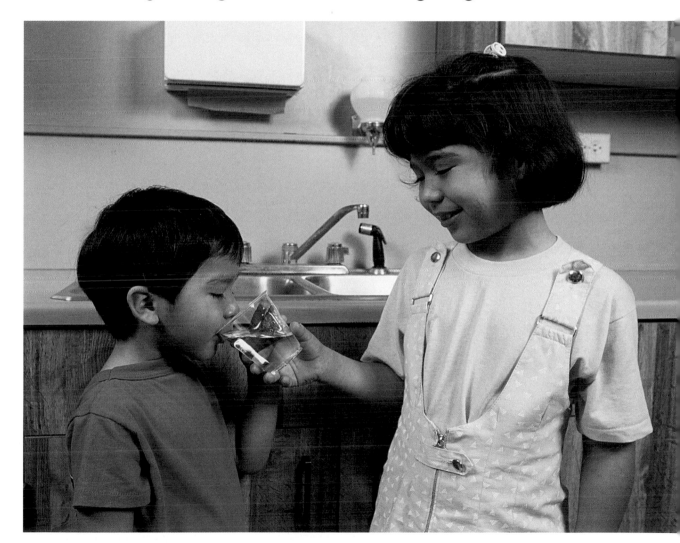

Healthy Nose and Throat

Your nose and throat help keep **germs** from making you sick. Your nose and throat have sticky insides called **mucous membranes.** These trap many germs that get in through your nose and mouth.

Sneezing and coughing are ways your body gets rid of trapped germs. Sneezing and coughing force germs out of your body. This helps keep you from getting sick.

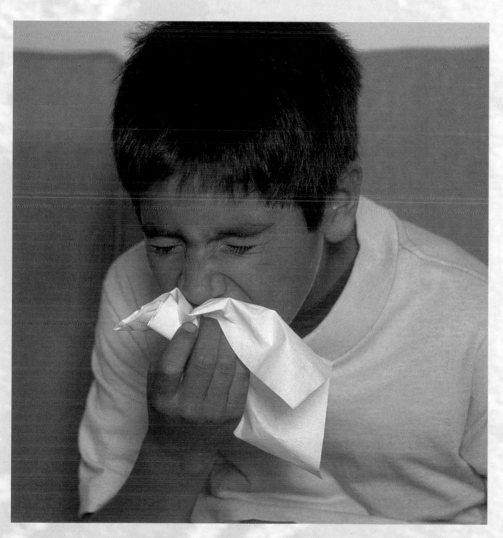

What Causes Mumps?

Mumps is caused by a **virus,** which is a
very tiny **germ.** The mumps virus is so
small you need a **microscope** to see it.
This is what the mumps virus looks like
through a microscope.

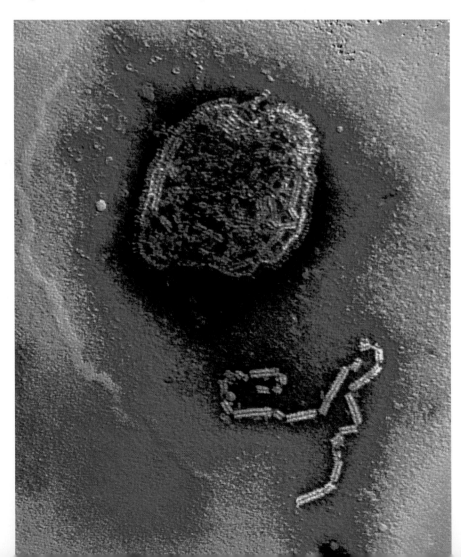

If the mumps virus gets into your body, it can make many more viruses. Then you get mumps. The virus gets into your **salivary glands,** which make **saliva.** These glands are just below and in front of your ears.

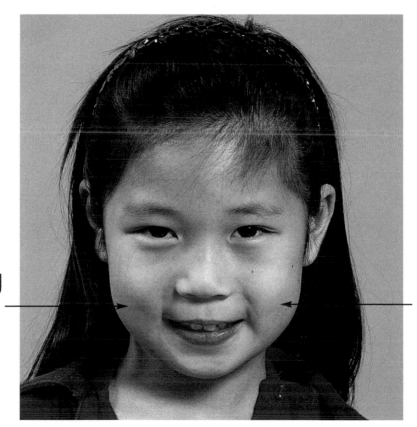

salivary gland — ← → — salivary gland

How Mumps Is Spread

The mumps **virus** lives in the nose, throat, and **saliva** of a person with mumps. The virus spreads when the sick person sneezes or coughs. Sneezing and coughing send the virus into the air.

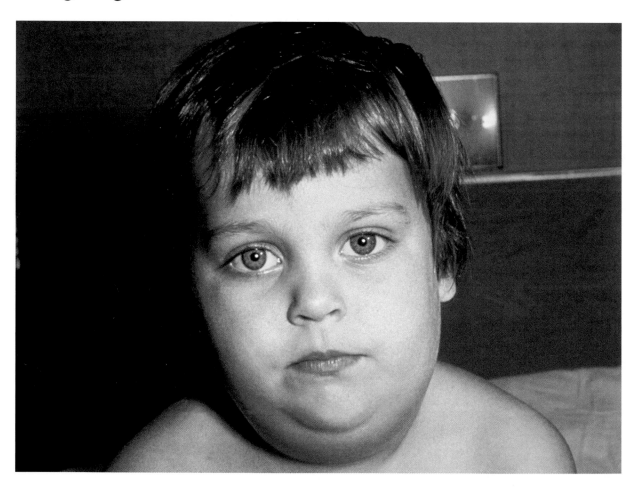

If you breathe in the virus after a person with mumps sneezes or coughs, you may get mumps. Mumps is **infectious** before and after the signs of mumps appear.

First Signs

It can take two to three weeks for the mumps **virus** to make you feel sick. The first signs of mumps are often an **earache** and a **fever.**

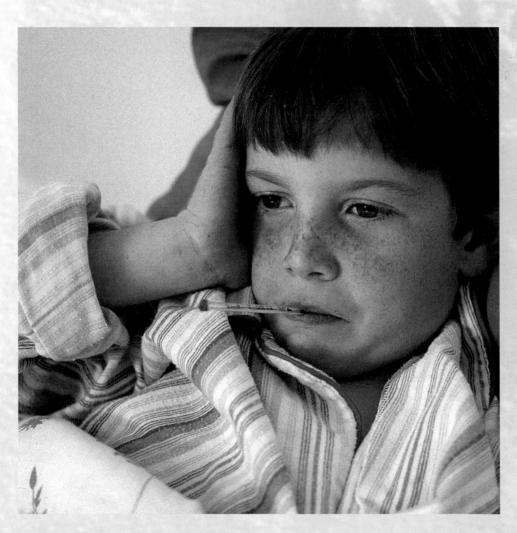

When you have a fever, your body **temperature** is hotter than normal. You may also feel tired and your head may hurt.

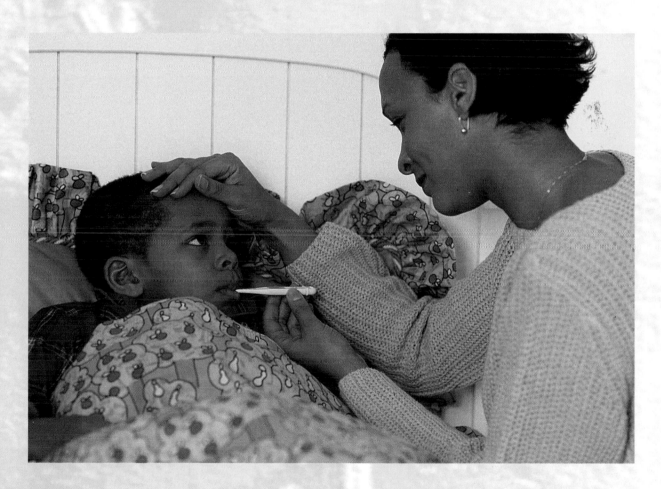

The Next Stage

Next, one or both of your **salivary glands** will **swell.** This causes your cheeks to puff out just below your ear and across your **jaw.**

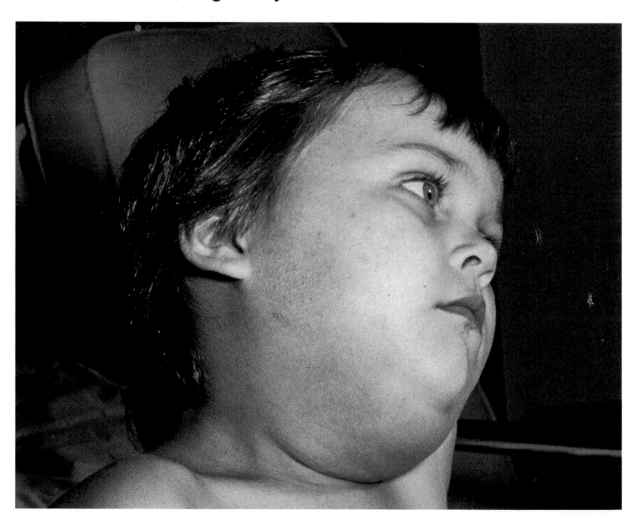

If you press on the puffy area, it will hurt. It may also hurt to chew. Many people with mumps do not feel like eating because it hurts when they chew.

Treatment

If you feel sick and your cheeks begin to puff out, you should go to a doctor. If the doctor says you have mumps, you need to stay home and rest.

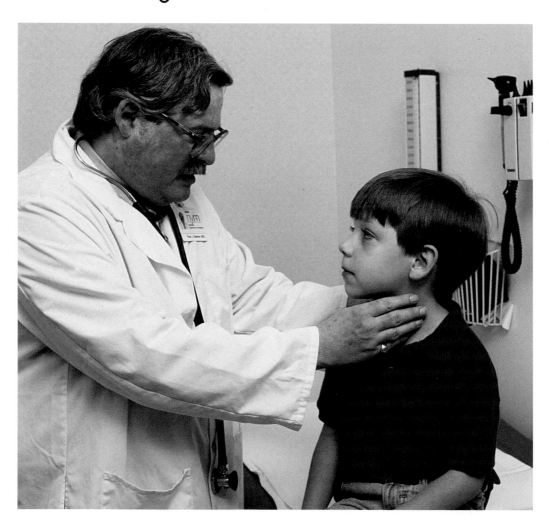

There is no medicine that will make mumps go away. Your body will fight the **virus** and get better on its own.

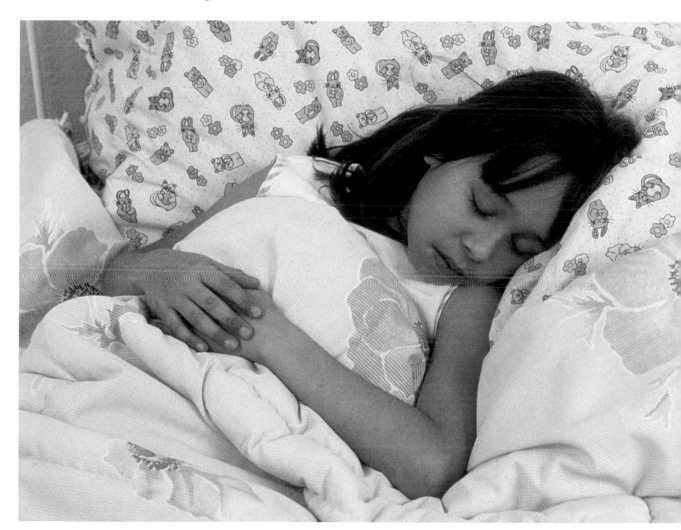

Feeling Better

You can put a cold, wet cloth on the parts of your face that hurt or are puffy. This will make them hurt less. An adult may also give you **pain relievers** to help you feel better.

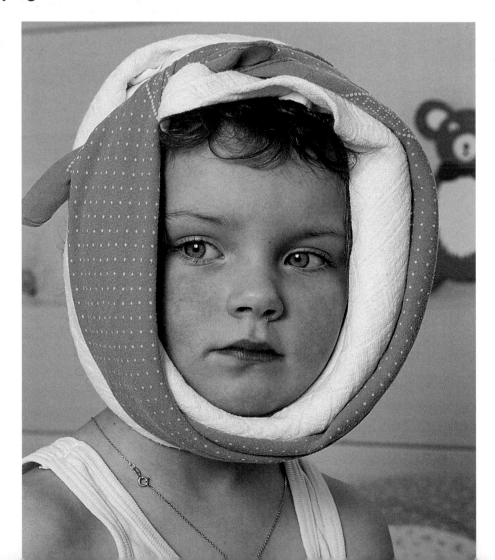

The puffy areas will start to go back to normal in about a week. In ten to twelve days you should feel well again.

When Mumps Is More Serious

For most people, mumps is not serious. But for a very small number of people, mumps sometimes causes deafness, or loss of hearing.

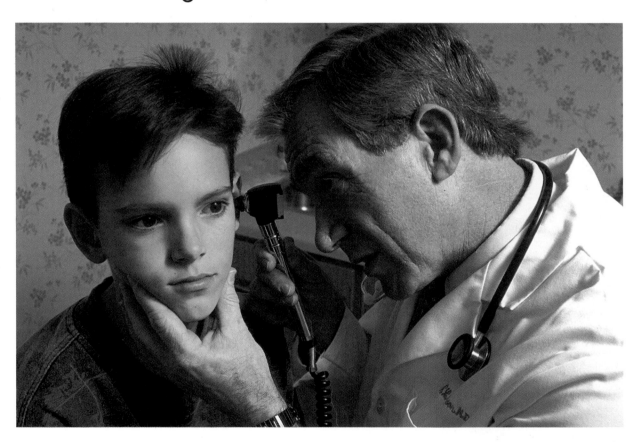

Signs that mumps is getting worse are a high **fever,** a very bad **headache,** and a stiff neck. People who have any of these signs should see a doctor.

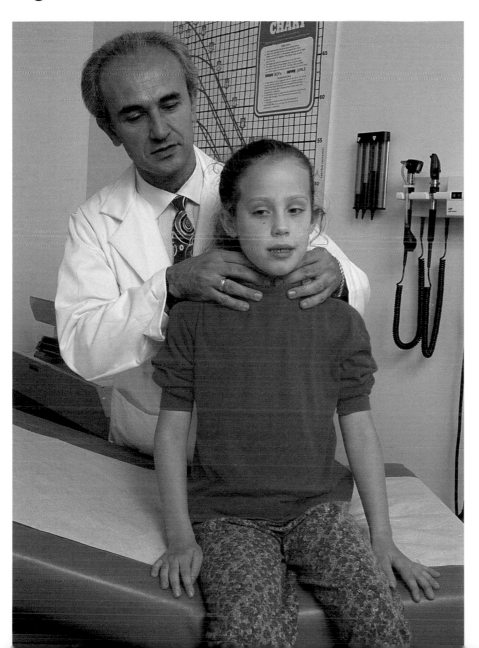

Avoiding Mumps

Many people get a mumps shot, or
vaccine, that keeps them from getting
mumps. Getting the vaccine gives people
immunity to mumps. This means they
cannot catch it.

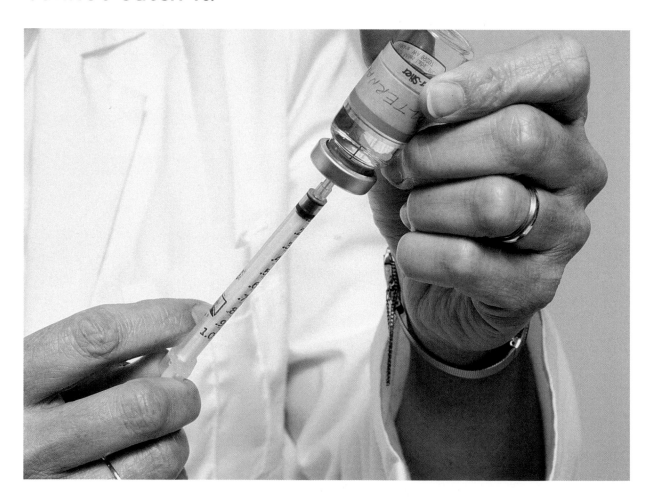

Before the mumps vaccine was invented, many children got mumps. Today, the vaccine keeps most children from getting mumps.

Getting a Mumps Vaccine

Babies get the mumps **vaccine** when they are about one year old. They will get another **dose** of the vaccine later, too.

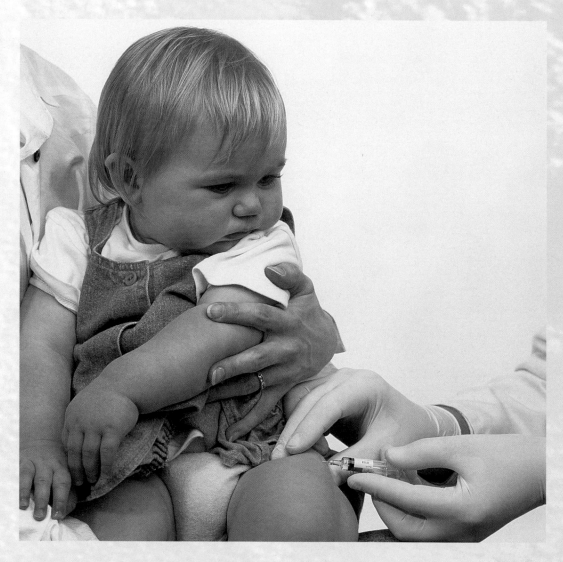

The extra dose is called a **booster shot.** Children get it when they are between the ages of four and six or between the ages of eleven and twelve.

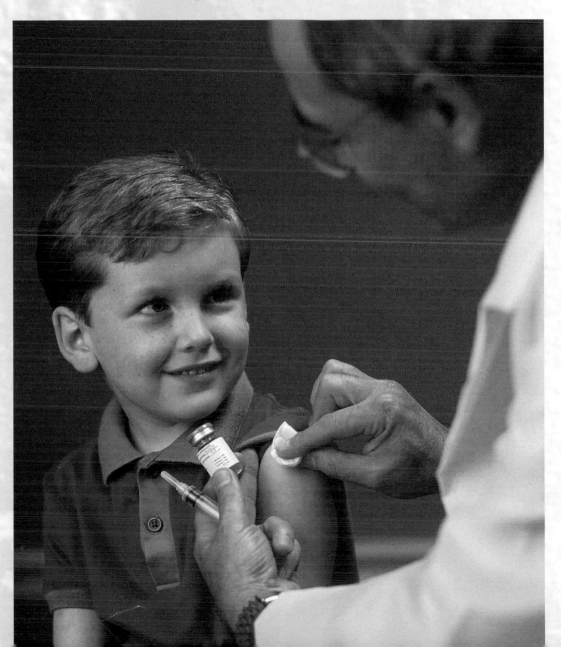

Staying Healthy

Once you have had mumps or the mumps **vaccine,** you will have **immunity** to mumps. Your body will make special **blood cells** like this one.

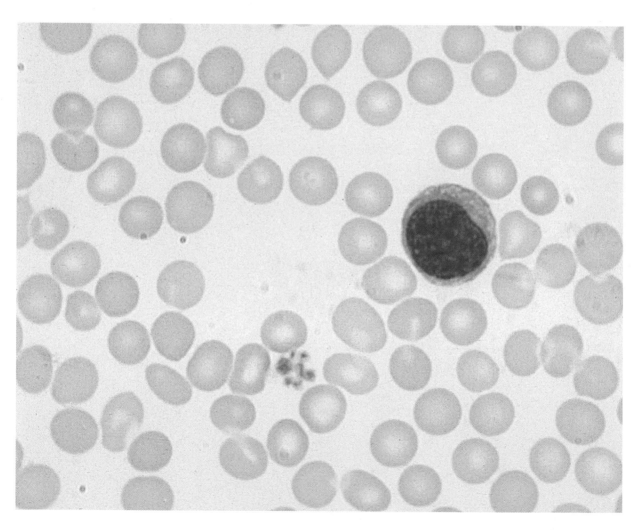

If the mumps **virus** enters your body, the special blood cells will protect you. They will attack the viruses and keep them from making you sick.

Think about It!

Tim had mumps last year. Now his sister has mumps. Can Tim catch mumps from her? Why or why not?*

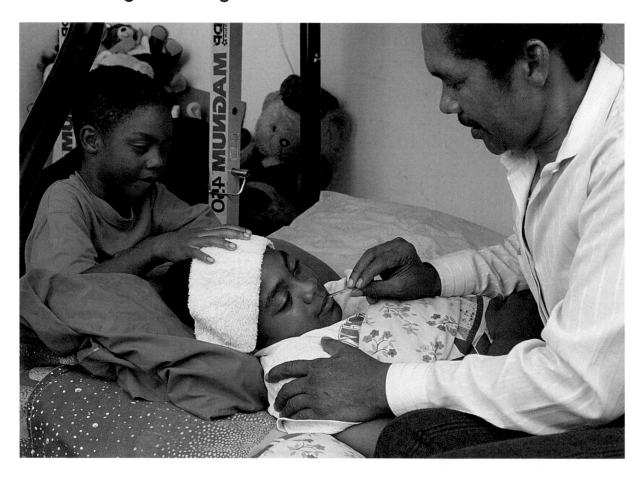

Jan has mumps. Her cheeks are very puffy and they hurt. What might make her feel better?*

*Read page 30 to find out.

Answers

Page 28

Tim cannot catch mumps from his sister. A person who has had mumps cannot get mumps again. Tim already had mumps, so now he has **immunity** to mumps.

Page 29

Jan could put a cloth soaked in cold water on her cheeks. Her parents might also give her **pain relievers** to help her feel better.

Stay Healthy and Safe!

1. Always tell an adult if you feel sick or think there is something wrong with you.

2. Never take any medicine unless it is given to you by an adult you trust.

3. Remember, the best way to stay healthy and safe is to eat good food, drink lots of water, keep clean, exercise, and get lots of sleep.

Glossary

blood cell   very tiny part of your blood

booster shot   extra dose of vaccine given at a later time

dose   how much you take of something, like a medicine

earache   pain inside the ear

fever   when the temperature of your body becomes hotter than usual

germ   very tiny thing that can make you sick if it gets in your body

headache   pain in or around the head

immunity   protection from getting an illness

infected   made sick or unhealthy by germs

infectious   can be passed from one person to another and can make you sick

jaw   lower part of the face

microscope   machine that makes very small things look big enough to see

mucous membrane   sticky inside of the nose and throat

pain reliever   liquid or pill that gets rid of pain

saliva   watery liquid made by the salivary glands

salivary gland   body part that is just under and in front of your ear that makes saliva

swell   get bigger

temperature   measure of how hot or cold something is

vaccine   shot that keeps people from getting a sickness

virus   very tiny germ that can make you sick if it gets inside your body

Index

More Books to Read

Hundley, David H. *Viruses.* Vero Beach, Fla.: Rourke Press, 1998.

Royston, Angela. *Clean and Healthy.* Chicago: Heinemann Library, 1999.

Saunders-Smith, Gail. *The Doctor's Office.* Minnetonka, Minn.: Capstone Press, 1998.